South American Horned Frogs as Pets

Facts & Information

South American Horned Frog General Info, Purchasing, Care, Cost, Keeping, Health, Supplies, Food, Breeding and More Included!

By Lolly Brown

Copyrights and Trademarks

Disclaimer and Legal Notice

Foreword

There have been countless people who have gone into the craze of raising frogs for so long that it can be safe to say that frogs have been an amphibian favorite in the reptile fancy for quite a while and there looks to be no letting up any time soon. The South American Horned Frog is a large colorful frog that sports a colorful body of green with dark red to black markings. Other South American horned frogs have color variations from tan and brown, green and brown as well as albino. They are such interesting little fellas, that we needed to let you in on the buzz.

Table of Contents

Introduction

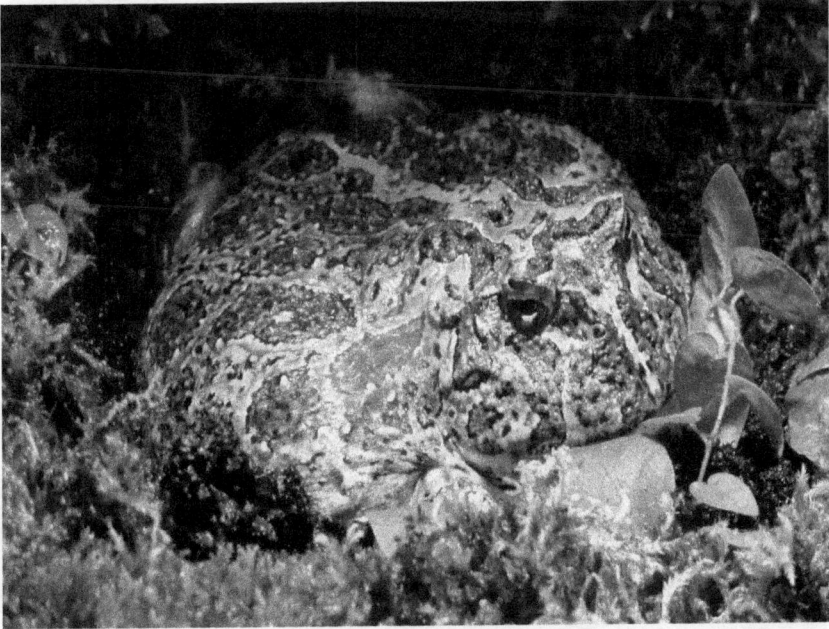

The South American horned frog, a well-known loner, is also known by a few names like the ornate horned frog, and the Pacman Frog. There are also a few of this frog specie with the enormous mouths which we shall be getting to know individually a little later on. A couple of them are highly popular in the reptile fancy. We shall be talking about them more here to find out what their needs are when in captivity. These large, usually silent frogs are some of the more favored in the amphibian category.

Introduction

These frogs are relatively big amphibians that come in a variety of amazing colors. Some have a yellow to stark green body coloration with red to almost black markings that run along their backs whilst others have different colors that is suitable for the habitat they live in. They have been given the nickname Pacman Frog because of their enormous mouths which practically take up their whole body.

These chilled out little guys are pretty good starter frogs for the novice and budding herp enthusiast to raise since they are not difficult to take care of as long as you know what to do. Here, we have compiled some of the most important things you need to know about taking care of these little frogs. Their needs are simple and their requirements few. If you remember to do the needful for these little guys you will understand the quiet joy of taking care of these little ones.

The South American Horned frog is an awesome amphibian that would be the perfect for anyone who likes quiet time bonding with their generally quiet pets. They are generally happy to just hang around in their tanks. We shall be looking into how you can set up enclosures for these magnificent frogs as well as all the important details you will need to understand how to care for these amphibians with confidence.

Chapter One: A Closer Look at the South American Horned Frog

The South American Horned Frog is a type of frog from the Ceratophryidae family. They are commonly called the Pacman frog because of their distinct disc shaped body and their enormous mouth that seems to take up a big part of their physique. They are great frogs to watch and study as they go about their usual days. They are the chill sort of frog that looks like a character from a children's story book.

You can tell the difference between a male and female South American horned frog by the sounds they make, or the absence thereof. The female South American horned frog will not be as vocal as their male counterparts. They will not croak or chirp as often as the male frogs. The male frogs are also set apart from the female population by way of their epidermis. The male South American horned frog will frequently be seen with spotted chests. The males would also develop spots on their finger pads upon maturity.

Physical Appearance

A baby South American horned frog can be as big as a quarter when you get it but it would later grow up to be quite a big sized frog upon maturity. It can grow to be as big as a small saucer, or the size of an adult person's palm! The South American horned frog is a good choice of frog specie for a new amphibian keeper. It does not need too much in terms of accessories so maintaining them, whether you get an individual frog or a couple of them, will certainly be a breeze as long as you know what you need and what to do.

This is not exactly the frog that likes to be held, so you will need to remember to keep handling to a minimum. Only handle South American horned frogs when absolutely necessary. We shall be going over more of the proper care and needs of the South American Horned Frog as we progress. In the meantime let's get to know them a little more.

Chapter One: A Closer Look at the South American Horned Frog

This frog is commonly known in the pet trade as the South American horned frog. Often times the frog that has a truly big mouth, is called the Pacman frog. The scientific name of this frog is the ceratophrys ornata. They are also known as the Argentine horned frog, the ornate pacman frog and the Argentine wide-mouthed frog. They grow up to about 6 inches long upon reaching adulthood and the female South American horned frogs are larger and bigger than their male counterparts. These frogs are about as long as they are wide, giving them that almost saucer-like shape when it is at rest.

Life in the Wild and in Captivity

In the wild, a South American horned frog could live up to about 5 years. This lifespan is dependent on how well of a hunter the frog is as well as how well it conceals itself from predators that would feed on them. When in captivity their chances of living longer lives increases as long as they are given the proper care and treatment they require. They thrive best in an environment that has loose substrate and where shallow water is present. They are quiet predators who lie in wait for their prey to come along. These frogs would commonly be found burrowed beneath the earth or contentedly be sitting in a small pool of water.

Chapter One: A Closer Look at the South American Horned Frog

The South American horned frog is not a great swimmer, but it does like soaking in water. Not only does the water keep them hydrated, it also helps their respiration. Their name says it all, and gives some indication of the habitat where they can be found naturally. Keep the room temperature between 75 - 80 degrees Fahrenheit. Make sure that the frogs are misted daily to ensure proper humidity.

These frogs are voracious eaters. In the wild, the South American horned frog would be seen dining on small fish, flies, mosquitoes, and other insects native to the area it lives They can be fed earthworms, crickets, phoenix worms, silkworms, and butter - worms. They may also be given the occasional mice, wax worm and a couple of guppies. They should not be fed super - worms or mealworms because of their hard, shell-like exterior. They are such hardy eaters that they would be able to gobble up a full grown rat! It is also not unusual to see one South American horned frog eat another of their kind.

Male vs. Female

Female South American horned frogs are generally bigger than their male counterparts. A mature female Argentine Horned Frog can easily eat a grown rat. These frogs, commonly found in Argentina, are also known to be cannibalistic. They are known to eat their mates, even if their mates are bigger than they are. It is highly advisable to isolate multiple frogs from each other.

These frogs are such voracious eaters that it wouldn't be odd to see them attempt to eat something larger than they are. They are known to be able to swallow animals that are half their size. They have a row of sharp bony projections for teeth located in their upper jaw. This feature of theirs makes it nearly impossible for these frogs to let go of their prey after they have it in their mouth. If this is not minded by the keeper of the frog this could lead to the choking to death.

These frogs who got their looks from the famous Pacman game, looks like it is all mouth when it eats. They have mouths as wide as their heads and they lunge at their prey, much like the hungry yellow disc of the famous arcade game. The ornate horned frog is one of the several species of horned frogs that are native to the tropical and montane rain forests. A few of the other species of ceratophrys can be found in more arid regions. These frogs are native to Northern Argentina, to Uruguay and the Rio Grande do Sul region of Brazil. They are carnivorous amphibians who grow to be very large frogs.

These amphibians grow at an exceptional rate, taking on their adult form just a couple of weeks after they hatch. From this point they continue to grow at a rapid rate. These frogs are often sold in the pet trade when they are no larger than a silver dollar and within a short five months these frogs will reach a size of six inches. From the time they are tiny little cornets to their adult size, these frogs are magnificent to observe and watch.

They are roundish in shape and have a plumpish physique. It is hard to tell where the head of the frog ends and its body begins because there is little demarcation to indicate. Their pupils are located high up in their eyes, adding to another similarity to the Pacman game.

The skin of the ornate frog effectively camouflages the frog when it lies half buried in dirt or fallen leaf piles. Their warty green, yellow and white skin, with a smattering of red and black flecks make for a perfect disguise when it is lying in wait for its next passing prey. The minute something comes within its limited, leaping range, it will make a go for it. Be it another frog, snake, a rodent, a lizard, a small bird or large insects, anything moving and in its general reach is free game. It only takes a couple of gulps for the South American horned frog to swallow its prey.

Chapter One: A Closer Look at the South American Horned Frog

So, You Want to be a Frog Keeper?

These amphibians are easy to care for as long as the person intending to raise them finds out what they need to do in order to provide for its maintenance. These frogs, like all other frogs sleep with their eye open. Some of them may be more active during the night time but they are usually diurnal frogs you can enjoy during the daytime. It is best to set up a room to house your frogs if you intend to keep more than one. Many frog keepers have seen the convenience of converting one of their rooms to a reptile/amphibian room. It is easier to keep a constant temperature grade this way. However, should you choose to keep just one of them, make sure that you have the necessary equipment that will keep the enclosure of your frog in the proper and temperate conditions it needs. We shall discuss more of setting up a terrarium for your frog later on.

Frogs are not like other pets that you can and should handle. Frogs have very sensitive skin and get easily contaminated by the oil we have in our hands. Its skin is a supplemental breathing organ for the frog and it is unwise to handle any pet frog unless absolutely needed. The oils our hands produce can be harmful to the frog, so it is important to wash your hands with clean, distilled water before you handle a frog, and do this only when needed, i.e. when you need to clean out their enclosure.

Chapter One: A Closer Look at the South American Horned Frog

Should you absolutely need to pick up a South American horned frog, be sure to pick it up from the back where it won't see your fingers. Many frog owners have experienced their fingers being mistaken for food. A typical human reaction would be to flick the offending frog. Keep your reactions to a minimum and try not to fling the poor thing across the room. South American horned frogs are aggressive and vicious. They live for food and will go for anything that moves anywhere near their mouths. Ornate frogs have no teeth to speak of, so if does happen to attach itself to your finger, give it a second or two to figure out that your tasteless thumb is unappetizing.

Chapter Two: Origin and Distribution

The South American horned frog grows up to be quite massive at a length of about 5.5 to 6 inches. They are plump, colorful frogs, who are often green with red and black flecks. Female South American horned frogs are bigger than their male counterparts and may weigh up to one pound. These frogs can be found living in burrows and muddy vegetation of the forest floors of Brazil, Paraguay, Uruguay and Argentina. There are currently not on any of the endangered lists of the IUCN, CITES or USFWS. These frogs from the south of the globe are hardy eaters of large insects, small lizards, mice and sometimes small birds.

Facts about the South American Horned Frog

These frogs are frequently touted as "mouths with legs" because their mouths appear to take up the entire front half of the frog's body. It is probably why it borrows its nickname from one of the greatest arcade games of the 1980's. Its common name, horned frog, is taken from the folds of its skin which are positioned just above its eyes, making them look like they have tiny horns on top of their heads.

The horned frog, as an adult, is a passive hunter. It lies in wait for its food to come to it. And when one is unfortunately in the general range of the frog, it lunges and it gobbles up the prey. Juvenile South American horned frogs are very active feeders and are cannibalistic, eating other frogs of the brood.

This species has teeth on the roof of its mouth called vomerine teeth. These are not so much actual teeth but more like protruding bones around the outside of its jaw that act as their teeth. They have very strong jaws that would instantly clamp down on anything that moves in front of their face. Often times, these frogs would accidentally swallow something that is bigger than they are. They would usually spit it out after discovering that it isn't tasty or something to eat, but there can be instances when the frog swallows an object. This is usually worked out by giving the frog laxatives.

Being a small predator, one of the South American horned frog's roles in the balance and order of things is controlling populations of small animals. Horned frogs themselves, as tadpoles and adults, are a source of food for many other carnivores they share their environment with. As with all amphibians, South American horned frogs have porous skin; their skin is a very sensitive organ that is vital to their survival. It responds quickly to changes in the environment; these frogs are very sensitive to minute changes in the ecosystem.

South American horned frogs are becoming very popular in the realm of scientific embryological research. Researchers are now able to cease the development of the egg during the different stages of its development in order to better understand cell division.

The scientific name of the South American horned frog is the Ceratophrys ornata. It is commonly called the Ornate Horned frog. In the pet trade, this huge frog from South America is lovingly called the Pacman frog. They are also commonly called the South American horned frog, the Argentine horned frog, the ornate Pacman frog, and the Argentine wide-mouthed frog.

In its adult state, the frog grows to about 6 inches long. The female South American horned frog grows larger than the male frogs. These frogs are about as wide as they are long. In the wild they are seen to live for up to about 4-5 years. In captivity, their chances of survival increases, and they are seen to live up to about 10 years.

These land - dwelling, or terrestrial amphibians are native to the regions of South America, and can be spotted in the forests of Uruguay, Brazil, Paraguay and Argentina. They are very poor swimmers and prefer to sit and lounge, spending most of their time, in the humid environment amongst the damp leaf litter of the forest floor.

The pacman frog has a really good appetite and it matches their size. They will pretty much eat anything that moves within striking distance. They typically spend their time sitting and waiting on the ground for the next big meal to come along. Any prey that walks by is fair game for this seemingly perpetually hungry frog.

Types of South American Horned Frogs

There are over 8 species of ornate frogs that range in various regions of South America. They are generally forest floor dwellers who like to burrow beneath the leaf piles. The South American horned frog is a great starter frog pet for a novice herp enthusiast. They make great companions and are awesome to observe.

The South American horned frog is native to the subtropical regions of southern Brazil, eastern-central Argentina, Uruguay and Paraguay. They are one of the larger frog species that are easy to find in the pet trade and is simple enough to get hold of. They are classified as a hardy frog species that has an average life span of 10-15 years, with proper care, under captivity. They grow to an average size of about 5.5 to 6 inches and they are as long as they are wide. When in rest, which is most of the time, you will soon discover, the South American horned frog looks much like a saucer.

Pacman Frogs come in a variety of amazing morphs. These awesome little-big frogs have colors ranging from albino to ornate color combos of yellow or green with flecks of red and black. This trait is one of the most endearing characteristics of this species, and a major reason they are so popular with amphibian hobbyists. They are one of the biggest frogs of the world and can sometimes reach up to 7 inches! They have a tendency to become pretty obese because of the inactivity of their lifestyle, so be careful how much you feed your South American horned frog.

These frogs have really wide mouths, so be careful wagging your fingers in front of its face. It will try to eat anything that they can get a hold of, and this includes your finger and bigger animals. You will want to house your South American horned frogs individually. Keep them away from each other as well as other frogs because only time will tell when one goes for the other.

They are great eaters and will eat crickets, earthworms, minnows, guppies, mice of appropriate sizes, as well as other insects.

Make sure that you give your South American horned frogs a balanced diet of insects and protein. Don't feed them a sole diet of mice because they can get fat from this too-rich diet, and ornate frogs are prone to obesity because of their lack of physical activity.

Keep in mind that large frogs need not be fat frogs. A responsible amphibian enthusiast would research the amphibian they plan to acquire before they actually bring one home. As you study more about the South American horned frog you will understand that there is a weight issue to consider, and yes, one can over - feed a Pacman.

You can handle a Pacman frog, but you should refrain from doing so unless absolutely needed. Should you need to handle a South American horned frog, you will want to make sure to wash your hands before and after handling it. Most frogs, especially the ornate horned frog, absorb things through its skin, therefore it could easily become irritated with the natural oils our hands produce, so you want to make sure that your hands are clean before handling.

With regard to hand washing after handling one, it is just as important to do this because frogs can have secretions that can irritate the eyes, nose, mouth, as well as any cuts or abrasions that the person may have.

Dangers Faced by the South American Horned Frog

The South American Horned Frog is presently a stable frog population and is listed status with the IUCN of "least concern".

Although the South American horned frog is not listed on any of the endangered species lists, there are threats to their natural environment. These pose grave danger to the frog's natural habitat. The thoughtless act of illegal logging, and the ever present threat of deforestation has limited the land area of their natural habitats are growing concerns, with countless hectares of land being razed for the land to be used for agricultural purposes.

This human intervention of the land it is natural to has gravely affected the habitation of many frog species. In fact, over 30 percent of the frog species of the world are listed as endangered. Their very existence is threatened by unscrupulous individuals who are easily lured with the promise of quick money. Should this trend continue, we shall have to deal with the slow extinction of many animals, insects and fauna but we also miss out on the many advantages and learning we can get from these living things that share our planet and are vital to the equilibrium of nature.

Chapter Three: Frog Supplies and Setting Up an Enclosure

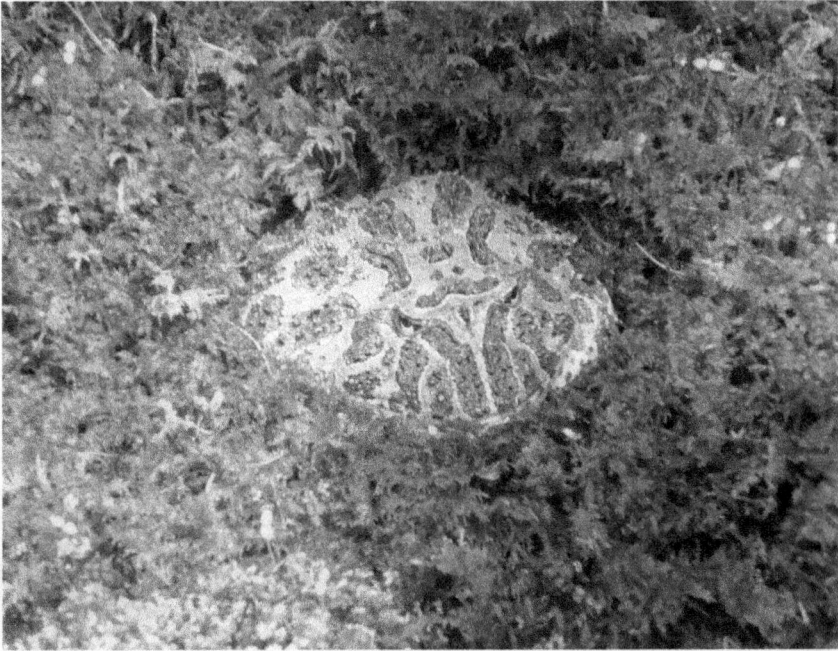

The enclosure is the most important piece of equipment the frogs you will be taking in, since they will be using this for their entire lifetime. We shall find out what we will initially need to set up a proper enclosure for our stoic buddy, the South American horned frog. We shall help you figure out the necessary sundries and equipment they will require to thrive and thrive well under your care.

Enclosure Size

The South American horned frogs are surprisingly big frogs that get rather large as they get older. They generally grow up to a maximum size of about 6 inches and look impressively massive upon reaching adulthood; some of them even grow to 7 inches. There aren't very the very active sort and you will often find them burrowed and sitting still. They aren't exactly the restless sort of frogs who need space to move. The South American horned frog can live well and be housed in a 10 or 20 gallon tank.

Keep in mind that these frogs are not social frogs and need to be housed alone in their own enclosure. Apart from its usual 10 to 20 gallon terrarium, your frog will also need a quarantine tank and a tank where you can house them temporarily during the monthly general cleaning of the frog's enclosure.

A baby pacman frog is about the size of a quarter, whilst a more mature Pacman frog could be as big as your palm. They are not exactly social frogs so keep this bit in mind when setting up their enclosure.

Their enclosure is only meant to be theirs alone. If you plan on taking in and raising more than one of these frogs, make sure that you provide them all with their own cages. Unless you are intending to breed your Pacman frogs you will not want to put them together in one enclosure, as they will attack each other. The bigger, stronger one will want the territory for itself so the weaker one will be in danger of being the other's dinner.

They will need a 5 to 10 gallon water-tight exo - terra tank to live comfortably. They don't need anything bigger because they spend most of the time in one place. Since they are opportunistic eaters and would usually lie in wait for their next meal, when in the wild. They are not the busy leapers and hoppers like other frog species, so they will not need too much in their tanks to keep them happy.

It is recommended that you use a loose substrate, like coco husk and moss works well. You will need to make sure that they can burrow down. They need to be able to have a place that would closely resemble their natural habitat. They are "sit and wait" predators who do not walk around a lot. However, it would be nice to add in a little greenery and foliage to their tanks because it does liven up the tank, for one, and these will provide the frog a little comfort and security - somewhere they can lounge and sit in wait.

They have very simple needs in terms of lighting and temperature. If you have a reptile room, then you will most probably have the room temperature at a stable 60-70 degrees.

Frog Supplies and Equipment

Frogs have an intricate respiratory system and their skin actually assists them in breathing and staying moist. Provide the South American horned frog with a soak dish where they can lounge and moisturize their skin. Make sure that this is a shallow dish where they just have enough depth to soak in.

Owners of these frogs would also sometimes notice their South American horned frogs to defecate in the soaking dishes. It is believed that these frogs will usually not defecate where they eat, so they may choose to go into the soak dish to pass waste. Be sure to check the dish at least twice a day to make sure that there are no feces festering in the water. Replace the water in the dish with fresh water each time.

Set up a proper terrarium that will not only promote a healthy environment but will also be conducive for the frog's good life. The terrarium you set up should be a place where the environment gives your new pet a shelter. If you do not have a reptile room, where the temperature is kept in the proper setting, you will need to get individual equipment to provide the proper lighting, heating and humidity.. It must be a space which will provide the right conditions in order for it to maintain good health.

Chapter Three: Frog Supplies and Setting Up an Enclosure

One adult frog can be kept in a 10 gallon glass tank. Choose a tank that has dimensions that is longer than it is tall. These frogs usually sit in one place for the duration of its day, so make sure it has enough floor space. Keeping a frog enclosure clean can be a lot of work. Many frogs have fairly simple light, temperature, and humidity requirements but they are very sensitive to contaminants and waste in their environment so make sure that you make it your job to clean out their enclosures at least once every month.

In the wild, frogs are just as concerned about being eaten by bigger animals as they are about feeding. Lessen the stress factor and cover the outside back of the tank to give the frog a sense of security. Now fill the aquarium with two inches of coconut fiber substrate which is a substrate mixture made from the husks of coconuts. This can be safely composted or recycled into potted plants or gardens. You can ask a vet or pet shop owner if you're not sure what these are or where you can find them. Use a mixture of sphagnum moss and coco fiber.

Some people may find frogs to be boring, since they can't usually be handled but there are a few workarounds to that issue. First of all, you can handle a South American horned frog and bring it with you to another room - just make sure that you have a clean place to set the frog on, like a clean blanket, or a shallow tank. You can bring it with you to the next room and watch a movie with it for a couple of hours. Just don't forget to put your frog back in the tank right after.

Adding some foliage can also help the humidity levels of the tank and driftwood can be used by your frog as a hide. You may use fake plants or you can also use live plants such as Ficus, the Hibiscus and Pothos. These plants pose no toxic threat to the South American horned frog. Do not use moss you find in your yard or random places since it could have parasites that could be harmful to the frog.

Put a shallow dish of clean water on one side of the tank where your frog can soak. It should be big enough for the frog to fit in with enough room for it to move around. Make sure that it is not too deep as South American horned frogs are not good swimmers.

Maintain enclosure humidity at around 50% and mist the enclosure at least once or twice a day. Doing so will provide the proper moisture level. Use a humidity gauge to help maintain the proper levels. Hand misters are usually sufficient but if you don't remember to mist, an automatic mister can do the job of remembering for you. You'll be spending a little extra money but it is a better investment than forgetting.

Purchase supplies from a pet shop and gather everything you would need to set up the terrarium. An all-new set up will depend on how imaginative you are and what you intend to include. You can also use a second hand tank but make sure you clean out the tank thoroughly first. Make sure that you sanitize it well.

- A 10-gallon glass terrarium will cost about $100-150

- A digital thermometer is roughly around $6-12

- A heaters is about $15.00

- UVB light is around $20

Chapter Four: Growth Rate, Physical and Behavioral Characteristics

A South American Horned Frog is a fast grower. It comes to its mature appearance around the 2nd week of life and is about the size of a quarter. The growth rate for these frogs is pretty quick, with them growing to their adult size in a short 5 month span. The adult South American horned frog is a large and heavy frog. The female South American horned frog or the Argentine horned frog grows to an average 6.5 inches and can weigh up to a pound. Its male counterpart is a tad smaller, measuring in at about four inches and weighing just a little under a pound. They are extremely strong amphibians with very powerful jaws.

Instead of teeth, the South American horned frog has little, bony, teeth-like projections lining their powerful jaws. Their jaws as well as the tiny, bony projections are all designed and meant to clamp on to a prey. They will gobble up anything that will come anywhere close to their leaping range. They will patiently wait and pounce at anything that moves and will hold on tight. They will even attempt to eat something bigger than themselves, so be careful that you supervise feeding time.

It has a mouth that is built for eating. The South American horned frog has a cavernous mouth that can fit in a number of small insects and bugs at the same time. The mouth of a South American horned frog can accommodate a multitude of invertebrates, at once. It can gobble up a small reptile in two quick gulps, as well as small mammals, like mice or rats, including other amphibians as well as its own kind.

These frogs have a mouth that extends back to nearly one third the length of the frog's body. This gives them an appearance of being nothing more than a head with legs attached at the back. The upper eyelids of the South American horned frog form a fleshy projection that juts out from the tops of its lids, giving it the horned look.
The *C. cornuta* have more pronounced horny projections, making them an amphibian favorite.

They come in a variety of color camouflage allowing them to conceal their presence. Their colors typically have hints of reddish brown, yellow, black, white and green and in combinations which naturally give a "classic military" camouflage look. Many private breeders have been able to define and isolate specific patterns and colors through selective breeding. These breeding programs have resulted in some of the most amazing living artwork on four legs.

Longevity/Lifespan

Their little bodies sponge up water from their bladder, making their movements (stool) have a semi-solid consistency. They are cool, calm and collected as they sit in wait amongst the leaf litter of the forest floor. They display very low activity level. Some of them are diurnal whilst others are more active during night time. You will soon get to know your frog buddy's own particular trait.

The average lifespan of a Ceratophrys frog in the wild varies between 1 and 4 years, though in captivity and as pets, depending on diet and care, they may live 6 to 10 years and even longer. The rules of nature dictate that these frogs live in areas where they are able to find food sources in order to thrive. The presence of other animals compromises the safety of the South American horned frog because of possible predation. This frog is a favorite food fare for predators and is prey to snakes, birds and other larger frogs. South American Horned Frogs keep the balance in the environment it exists.

Keeping the South American Horned Frog Healthy

A South American horned frog, in the wild, has tendency to illnesses that may in turn contaminate the soil and water source. With thoughtful care during captivity, the odds of the frog improve. Diligent maintenance and keen observation is primarily what allows the South American horned frog to thrive well in captivity.

They are hardy, and resilient little guys that have been reported to live lengthy lives of up to 15 years under the meticulous care of an experienced and watchful keeper. Provide the frog with proper housing conditions and give it a place to live as it would in the wild - removing them from any danger. Set up for them a terrarium that would provide your South American horned frog all the perks of being in their natural habitat.

Provide your South American horned frogs with the necessary food they will need and you will soon realize how quickly these frogs grow. They are hardy eaters and feeding time is actually a joy to watch and observe.

Above all, make sure that you keep the cleanliness of the tank your South American horned frog is housed in clean. Maintaining tank and enclosure cleanliness is the key to raising a healthy frog. Keep in mind that most illnesses and diseases contracted by living beings, most especially captive pets, begin in improper husbandry or unsanitary habitat.

Chapter Four: Growth Rate, Physical, and Behavioral Characteristics

Chapter Five: Breeding South American Horned Frogs

The Argentine Horned Frog is a frog that occurs naturally in the moist grasslands of Argentina in South America. These frogs can grow to an impressively massive size of about 7 inches. They spend most of their lives buried halfway deep in soft, moist soil. They are ambush predators who are opportunistic eaters. They are frogs with great big appetites and will lunge at anything moving in front of their face. Their horned skin along with their sometimes yellow, sometimes green, other times, brown sin, flecked with red and black, make for good camouflage on the forest floor.

South American Horned Frogs are quite easy to breed when in captivity. Before breeding the mating pair will have to go on 60-day hibernation. During hibernation you will want to place the frogs in a cool and dry environment. Laying of eggs and the hatching of them should follow a few days after.

Mating and Breeding

South American horned frogs breed fairly easily in captivity. You will only need to follow a simple yet specific conditioning routine along with a healthy mating pair, and you should be set. Make certain that your South American horned frogs are well-fed and hydrated Just ahead of the winter months. They should have had a week or two to fully digest the food they consumed and pass along any solid waste, emptying their stomachs.

You will need to gradually reduce the temperature of the reptile room or the mating tank by 5 to 10 degrees. This temp grade can often be achieved by relocating the horned frog's tank closer to the floor. Upon reducing the temp in the tank, you will need to stop feeding and watering your frogs completely.

As the substrate in the mating frog's tank becomes increasingly dry, you will notice the frogs burrowing deeper into the substrate. This is when the frog will begin to develop a dry sac over its body. When the substrate becomes completely dry so will the frog be dry. The membrane sac will prevent water loss from the frog to the surrounding substrate. Leave your frogs alone and avoid from disturbing them for the next two to three months.

After this brief dry dormancy you may gradually moisten the substrate again until it is thoroughly and evenly moistened. The frogs will begin to appear from their burrow feeling refreshed. They will then consume their moisture retention membrane. Start offering food to your South American horned frogs again as you maintain a routine of misting the frog's enclosure heavily several times a day.

After several days of generous misting, transfer your frogs into a rain chamber. This is where your male will begin courting the female frog. A rain chamber can be built with relative ease. There are available instructions online and often suggests the use of a plastic tub filled with shallow water, a few artificial plants which eggs can be attached to, and a source of heat to maintain a steady water temperature. You will also need to provide a landing area, like as a smooth stone to accommodate tired frogs.

Males begin to develop a darkened area beneath the throat when they reach adulthood. They use this to call out to females by using an odd low toned clinking sound. It sounds a lot like a rusty bolt being manipulated with a rusty nut.

Upon placing the frogs into a rain chamber, the prepared and conditioned males will mount the receptive females and wrap the female in an embrace called the amplexus. This embrace may last for a span of several days or until the females deposit eggs to be fertilized by the male's own genetic material.

Once eggs have been laid and fertilized, the mating, adult frogs have to be removed from the rain chamber. Return the mating individuals to their regular captive tanks. Water has to be added to the rain chamber tub which contains the eggs. The fertilized eggs should be ready to hatch in four to seven days. Keep tadpoles on a diet of flaked fish food and algae. As soon as the tadpoles have matured into actual froglets, you will need to provide housing for each froglet to avoid cannibalism.

Steps to Breeding

- Identify a female and male South American horned frog. Keep in mind that a female South American horned frog will be about 1 to 3 inches bigger than the male

- Place the mating pair in a tank that is layered with a substrate of sphagnum moss.

- Maintain the temperature in the tank around 70 degrees Fahrenheit.

- Provide the pair with a shallow water bowl. DO NOT spray or mist the tank.

- Keep the mating frogs in this environment for a period two months.

- Transfer the frogs to a tank filled with shallow water, just enough water that the frogs can rest on the bottom and still breathe.

- Place aquatic plants in the tank where the female can attach eggs.

- Set up the breeding tank to provide the frogs an area out of the water that they can easily access.

- Spray the frogs with water multiple times each day to simulate rain and the female should lay eggs within days.

- When the female frog has laid her eggs on the plants you have places in the breeding tank, you will want to return the frogs to their individual and usual tanks.

- Add water to the tank that contains the eggs.

- These eggs should hatch shortly, about 3 days.

- Once the tadpoles hatch, you will want to separate each of the tadpoles and put them in their respective tanks. This will avoid any cannibalism amongst the tadpoles.

Social Structure and Behavior

Upon maturity and most, notable during mating season, male South American horned frogs will start to produce nuptial pads. This is a spot located at the inside of each thumb. They are vocal during the night, sending out calls for a few hours. Frog calls are more apparent and last longer at the height of the rainy season, which is also the time of year they breed. The males would call out and be heard several miles away.

During mating period, or when the environment is simulated for breeding, a short ritual of courtship begins. If the female is satisfied by what she sees, she will do a 90 degree turn, making way for the male. The male would then climb on to the back of the female. With the male on her back, the female would then begin to crawl along the forest floor in search of suitable leaf that is near water and is broad enough to accommodate a payload of eggs. Once the mating couple finds the proper conditions for the eggs to thrive they would lay up to 1,000 to 2,000 eggs.

Chapter Six: General Requirements and Reminders

The horned frog is a favorite among amphibian keepers primarily because of their compact size and stature. They are also favored because they do not require much space and is happy to find a spot and sit there. These hearty eaters are popular because of their voracious appetites. Whatever sort of housing environment you choose to provide for your frogs, be sure that you keep them clean and maintain cleanliness. You will also want to cover the enclosures of your frog with mesh screen to prevent possible escapes (highly unlikely) and unwanted visitors (quite likely).

South American horned frogs do not particularly enjoy being handled nor would there be a reason for you to handle them like you would a dog. Handling one can make the frog become quite stressed especially if the handling is done frequently. Should there be a need for you to handle your South American horned frogs, make sure that you wash your hands thoroughly, with water, to avoid contaminating the frog with the natural oils our skin produces. However, there will be occasion that will need you to handle the frog, like when you need to clean out its enclosure. When you do need to handle your frog, make sure that you do so with moistened, cupped hands. Cup the frog in your palm and cover it with your other hand lightly. This cupping action will reduce the likelihood of your frog lunging free from your grasp.

Be careful when you reach for your South American horned frog. They might just mistake your digits for food and attempt to gobble you up. Stay calm if this happens. Its bite may pack more of a shock than a punch, but it would still be unpleasant. South American horned frogs, though not aggressive, have a tremendous feeding reflex, so keep that in mind and mind your digits.

Temperature Range

Brazil, Argentina, Uruguay and Paraguay are regions of South America with complex weather patterns as well as contrasting micro climates, so these frogs in nature are able to balance out the temperature and humidity levels according to its natural surroundings.

Summers can be quite warm with a good portion of rainy days; winters in these regions are cooler and often very dry. Maintain your South American horned frogs at temperatures of about 75 - 80 degrees Fahrenheit, keeping it slightly cooler throughout the winter of about 70 degrees Fahrenheit.

The captive environment of the South American horned frog is not a complex one. They require no more than a safe enclosure from as small as a 5 gallon tank to a bigger 10 gallon tank, some proper substrate that will not irritate the frog's skin, and more importantly the weekly clean up as well as the monthly general tank cleaning. Keep in mind that these frogs are burrowers so make sure that you factor in the cost of replacing substrate when you work out the finances.

Substrate Options for Maintaining Temperature

Some substrate options for the South American horned frog's tank can be a mixture of moist peat moss, ground pine bark mulch or even clean soil. Careful steps should be taken to keep the substrate damp but not too wet. Too much water can develop to bacterial issues that in turn will lead up to illness.

- Keep your South American horned frogs in dampened soil or pine bark mulch. Allowing the soil to become quite dry before you spray to remoisten it.

- Pine bark mulch and soil both dry out from above, and works downwards as the top of the soil becomes completely dry, this is when you should mist the substrate again. These horned frogs seem to like and enjoy a light daily misting. Mist your frogs using a spray bottle early in the morning or late in the evening.

- It is extremely important that the frog's enclosure be kept clean. Do this by changing the substrate twice a month. Doing so will greatly reduce the chances of bacterial issues related to ammonia and fecal buildup.

- You can choose to leave a shallow body of water in the tank for your frogs. It isn't absolutely necessary. South American horned frogs get most of their moisture needs via perfusion through the soft tissues of their belly and cloaca. They will often hydrate when the tank is saturated again after a drying out period.

- Soak the South American horned frog in warm, shallow water at least once a week. If you are going to use a water bowl for the frogs, be sure to choose a shallow dish. A deep bowl will not only be difficult for your frog to climb into, it will also be difficult for the frog to get out. This may be a possible cause of accidental death if it cannot get back out.

- Let water stand open for a couple of hours before you put it on your frog's tank or use it on them. Letting it stand open will help reduce the chlorine levels and will be less stressful to the sensitive skin of the frogs.

Feeding South American Horned Frogs

South American horned frogs can be fed small, frequent meals comprised of soft bodied insects and worms.

They can also be offered the occasional vertebrate food items such as appropriately sized mice. Keep in mind that just because the South American horned frog has the capacity to swallow big food items; it doesn't mean it has to or should. First of all they could have a difficult time swallowing and aside from this, South American horned frogs are very inactive frogs. They often relocate to another location after defecating in their former spot. They hardly move, so feeding them a frequent diet of small mice can make them obese.

A variety of invertebrate food items several times a week is always best. Limit feeding them mammals to only once a week. These frogs should ideally have separate enclosures to avoid cannibalism. If you do decide to keep a few together in a big tank, make sure that they are all the same sizes. Also, keep a regular feeding schedule so as no one figures any of their other tank mates as dinner.

Chapter Seven: South American Horned Frogs as Pets

The South American horned frog is a massively roundish frog with an equally massive mouth. Some of them come in yellow skin tones with beady eyes that appear to have horns growing out of them. They are truly eager eaters and will not hesitate to try to take in something that might be bigger than they are. They are not the social kind and would fare best if kept in separate tanks from each other or other frogs. These frogs grow big and grow fast. From being no bigger than a quarter two weeks into its existence, the South American horned frog will quickly grow and reach its ultimate size within a short half year span of time.

There will be terrarium maintenance to be done so they are not the sort of frogs you would gift to a young child who does not have the proper knowledge of taking care of frogs. However, this can be a teaching point for young children at home. Remember that children should not do any heavy or complicated work that would directly expose them to the frog. Oils secreted in human skin as well as the secretions of the frog can have adverse effects on both parties.

These amazing frogs grow to quite an impressive size upon maturity. The largest measured female came in at 7.7 inches long as it is wide. These guys come out interested in one thing and that is filling its belly - as tiny tadpoles, they would gobble up another tadpole, so be sure to keep all the tadpoles, if you decide to breed these frogs, in separate tanks to avoid cannibalism. Under optimal conditions, these hardy frogs can live up to 15 years in captivity.

They are 'sit and wait' predators who would patiently lounge in their burrow, unmoving and hidden from curious eyes, only to come to life and pounce on a prey that was unfortunate enough to be in its leaping path. It is a quick movement that is over in the blink of an eye and is still a fascinating sight for many of the owners of these frogs.

Pros and Cons of Owning One

Amphibians in captivity faced grim chances of survival living with humans, before. Our lack of understanding of how they lived, what they ate, how they reproduced - these were things we were not aware of therefore we did not know how to take care of them. Since the surge of amphibian and reptile owners have increased in the recent decades, urgency for more herp experts increased as well. The advances of herp medicine have sped up exponentially since then, and with this new development our amphibious buddies stand a better chance of survival in captivity.

It is still not as easy to locate a herp vet. This is why it is really important to find one early on before bringing one home. Get in touch with your local herp society. They may be able to help you locate medical professionals who practice near you so make sure to network with other herp enthusiasts. Networking with other will allow you to reach out to others when you are in doubt. You can help others as well by sharing best practices.

The potential keeper is has to have a realistic understanding of what is expected of them as an amphibian keeper. Ask yourself honest questions about whether you are ready, able and willing to take on the responsibilities of being a pet owner and supply honest answers. A pet takes up time and costs money; are you up for these responsibilities? You will have to switch up your schedule to fit them in your day.

These frogs are amusing little fellas to watch when they go about doing what they naturally do. The tasks of cleaning out their tanks, maintaining the necessary temp and humidity levels, checking the substrate and feeding them could help you relax from the usual daily grind.

This species is not listed as endangered on the IUCN Red List. This means they are available for sale and it isn't hard to locate a couple of them if you know where to look. Although not the frog you would normally handle, the South American horned frog is a beautiful animal to watch. Witnessing the transitions they go through as they mature is a sight to see indeed. Feeding time is quite a treat to watch, seeing the natural instincts of the South American horned frog take over. Given the proper housing requirements they are a hardy bunch of amphibians that can be a source of great knowledge.

Chapter Eight: Diseases and Health Requirements

South American horned frogs generally a hardy, healthy species of frogs, but just like all animals, even these frogs can get or develop an illness, A number of factors are at play when considering the health of a South American horned frog. First of all, where you purchase a frog will greatly matter. The way you house the frog as well as what you feed them also all come into play.

You will want to make sure that you pay extra care about keeping the enclosure of the frog clean and that the diet of your horned frog is correct. Most common illnesses frogs get are usually directly related to improper housing, incorrect temperatures, poor water, dirty or unsuitable

substrate, or deficiencies in vitamins and/or minerals.
Consult with an experienced herp vet to help you
understand how to keep a South American horned frog
healthy. A herp vet can give you better insight on the needs
of the frog.

Metabolic Bone Disease

This is a common disorder seen in cold blooded pets
in captivity. This is a disease that causes soft bones and
deformities with the skeletal system. It will be important
that the food of the animal (reptile or amphibian in captivity)
be supplemented with calcium or calcium + D3. Not doing
so to a captive frog will lead to the possibility of it
developing metabolic bone disease. You will notice
indications of the illness if you see one or a few of the
following symptoms:

- a droopy lower jaw

- it fails to capture prey

- you'll notice muscle twitching

- the frog is listlessness

- backbone and pelvic deformities

MBD can be treated with the consistent coating of prey you feed the frog with calcium and vitamin D3. There are powder forms of this vitamin/mineral that you can ask your herp vet about. If the frog begins to display having problems of grabbing at prey because of its malformed or weak bones, you will want to administer calcium + D3 with a syringe by way of the frog's mouth. Carry this out once every 1-2 days until the bones start to harden.

Frogs can contract sickness and develop diseases for a number of reasons. Take stock of what you are in control of and make sure that these basic needs are kept satisfied to ensure the frog's longevity.

Toxic Out Syndrome

You have to make sure that the water inside the tank of your frog is changed frequently, because frogs absorb water through their skin from the substrate of the water bowl. If foul water is left to sit, and if this comes into contact with the frog or the substrate, the toxins can be absorbed by the frog's skin, which can develop to toxic out syndrome.

Indications of toxic out syndrome include can be recognized through one or any combination of the following:

- erratic jumping

- spastic extensions of the hind limbs

- listlessness

- cloudy eyes

Treat toxic out syndrome in frogs by putting it in a shallow water dish of clean water. Leave the frog there. You will have to replace the water every 4 hours until the signs of the illness go away. Avoid this by monitoring the conditions of the tank. Keeping the proper temp and humidity levels can prevent this from happening.

In the wild, amphibians and reptiles compensate for their vulnerability to bigger, stronger prey, by not showing weakness or indications of illness. This is a trait they carry with them even in captivity and often times give no indication of illness until it is too late. It is important you visit with your new routinely. Make these visits count by getting to know each of your pets. This will only be possible if you both spend time with each other. To an untrained eye, reptiles and amphibians seem like they all share the same traits and behaviors, but an experienced herp keeper will be able to distinguish one from another because of characteristic indications of each individual pet.

Water Edema Syndrome

A frog will start to swell up due to water retention. In extreme cases, the frog may even feel like a squishy water bag. Common causes of water edema are a damaged lymph heart and kidney disease. Up to now, experts are stumped as to how this can be prevented. Currently, there is no information on what to do to prevent this disorder. Limit the amount of water that you leave out for it. In severe cases, a vet can release the retained water by making small incisions at the affected sites.

An experienced herp vet will be the best person to tell you about the health of your frog. They are also the best people to give it a clean bill of health. Avoid the avoidable illnesses by keeping proper tank maintenance as well as providing the frog with the proper nutrients it will need. Keep a clean tank because poor and unsanitary conditions are the culprit of illnesses for reptile and amphibian pets. Poor enclosure conditions breeds a host of bacteria and viruses that affect the health of any pet.

Bacterial Infections

Frogs are normally exposed to bacteria but this is fought off by the immune system of the frog. If the frog's body is stressed, the immune system weakens giving way to bacterial infection. Stressful conditions can be identified through:

- constant presence of foul water

- improper temperatures

- overcrowding

Any of these situations can weaken a frog's immune system; therefore you want to make sure that proper husbandry is carried out to reduce the risk of stress. Signs of bacterial infections are different but can include:

- loss of appetite

- listlessness

- cloudy eyes

- Redness on the underside of the belly and the thighs

- Excessive skin sloughing with shed skin released in the water.

If the disorder goes unnoticed, extreme neurological signs may start to manifest. A herp vet can prescribe antibiotics or tetracycline baths or a combination of both. The baths have been seen to be more stressful and generally seen as ineffective.

Red leg is a common bacterial infection that can be fast and deadly. Dirty water, soiled substrate, and low temperatures can be the cause of the onset of the pathogen that causes red leg.

Despite all your good care, a frog could still get sick or it could get injured. Determining that there is something wrong with your frog will mean you know to recognize when something is amiss. This is why visiting with your frog regularly is important. Getting to know them will tip you off of any unusual behavior.

Fungal Infection

Fungal infections can infect wounds or scrapes, most common for tadpoles. Fungal infections can be treated topically. First you want to remove the frog from the water. You then want to get a cotton ball and soak it in mercurochrome, hydrogen peroxide, or malachite green. Daub the cotton ball on the affected area.

Endoparasites

Parasites are common among frogs and toads. Such parasites like roundworms, tapeworms, and pinworms. If you think that your frog has parasites, consult a veterinarian to diagnose and treat it before it is too late. Parasites are communicable if you have more than one frog in the same enclosure. This is why you it is strongly recommended that new amphibians coming into the mix be quarantined before being introduced to other pets. A herp vet will be able to give you the proper recommendations to keep your pet frogs healthy. They are the best people to prescribe and administer medication, if needed. Never medicate an ill pet on your own. You should not use human medicine as it may pose danger to the frog.

Blindness

Blindness is caused by a buildup of lipids on the corneas that is triggered by a diet that is high in fat. An example of a high-fat diet is pinkie mice as a staple diet. There is no cure for blindness but it can be potentially prevented with a low-fat diet.

Impaction

A frog can ingest some of the substrate when it lunges to grab a prey. Small gravel is usually released through the feces, but larger grains of gravel can remain lodged in the frog's intestinal tract which in turn causes blockage. Prevent impaction by housing the ornate frog on alternate substrates. If you suspect your frog is impacted, feel the belly, if there's a hard lump, it is probably substrate that the frog couldn't pass. The frog will usually excrete the substrate over a period of a few weeks. If the condition does not subside, consult a veterinarian to have it removed.

Bring your new frogs to the vet before taking them home. As a new and responsible herp keeper you have to understand the importance of quarantine. This measure of foresight spares other existing pets from being contaminated with virus that may be carried by a new arrival.

Obesity

These frogs grow large upon maturity. You would think they ate like a sumo. In fact, they require relatively little food to maintain a healthy weight. These are already big frogs, whether you feed it more is just unhealthy. Ornate frogs reach full size by about 2 - 3 years, the extra food that they consume upon reaching maximum body size, is converted to fat rather than bone or muscle. To prevent obesity, follow a feeding schedule.

- **Froglets up to 2 inches:**

    o Feed it with supplemented 3-week old crickets every 1-2 days

- **Froglets from 2 to 4 inches:**

    o Feed it with supplemented 3-week old crickets

    o pre killed pinkie mouse dipped in calcium

    o Supplement it with superworms in a shallow dish every 2 - 3 days.

- **Adult frogs up to 4 to 5 inches:**

    o Feed it with supplemented crickets or superworms in a shallow dish

    o You can also do a combination of both, night crawlers, or a pre killed/weaned mouse every 7 - 10 days.

Be sure that you have a carrier that will keep your pet safe during transport at any given time when needed. Having one ensures your pet and you are both safe from unexpected surprises between destinations. Make sure to invest in a lasting one because it will come in very handy, doubling up to be used as a safe holding place when you have to clean out the frog's terrarium.

Chapter Nine: Avoiding Illness and Care Sheet

What you need to look out for if you suspect your frogs to be ill are indications that are unusual of its typical appearance and habits. Get to know each of the frogs under your care. A frog that gets to you healthy from the beginning could be a good indication of things to come. Make sure that you get your frog from a reputable breeder who will be able to give you a guarantee. You will play a big role in the good health of your frogs. Should you notice change, or if it begins to manifest signs, or act funny, take it for a trip to the vet.

The culprit to reptile and amphibian illnesses often stem from one reason or a combination of wrong temperatures, the presence of nitrites or ammonia in the water, and dirty substrate. Other stress factors can be excessive light exposure or overcrowding. All these contribute to a depressed immune system in amphibians leading to them getting ill.

Be diligent and watchful of the necessary temperature, lighting, humidity and misting levels. Correcting these wrongs often causes frogs that show signs of sickness, to become healthy once more.

Should your pet frog continue to display symptoms of illness, get immediate veterinary care. Because there are such few practitioners of herp medicine, veterinary treatment for one frog can be quite costly with basic exam costing way over the cost of the frog. Therefore, do what is necessary to avoid costly bills.

To ensure the good health and long life of your pet amphibians, carefully fashion a terrarium that is regulated with the temperature, the correct humidity levels, optimal water quality, proper lighting, and clean furnishings. Make sure that the diet given to they meet the needs dietary needs of the frogs.

Check the accuracy of tank conditions on a routine basis. Doing so will prevent the onset of diseases. New animals will have to be kept separately from established pets and quarantined before being given a tank. Here are some indications that your frog is sick;

- Abnormal behavior

- A change of physical appearance.

- Extended soaks in the water

- A sudden or gradual weight loss apparent in the belly area, stomach appears hollow with hip bones and backbones more prominent, skin is saggy.

- Abdominal bloating caused by extreme digestive gases associated with poor digestion.

- Red blotches on the skin, due to hemorrhaging

- White fuzzy blotches due to fungal infection.

- E ye cloudiness: the eye lens is usually the first to be affected by pathogens when a frog's immune system is weak

- Edema is a general swelling of the frog's body, head, or limbs.

- Inadequate water quality, bacterial infections and kidney disease, are some some causes that trigger edema.

- Cloudy eyes are commonly secondary to other unseen problems.

- Your frog may have diarrhea if you notice more droppings. Bring it to the vet.

- Not eating is one symptom that could indicate a problem exists or it could be a sign that it is bored with the food it is given.

- When a usually active frog is ill it becomes listless.

- If your frog or toad hardly reacts to your touch it is almost certain that it may be sick.

- If it seems to have difficulty moving about, then take it as a sure sign of a problem.

- Injuries are another cause for odd behavior

- A frog that constantly yawns may be a sign of spring disease. Go to the vet.

- If it is not defecating then there has to be a problem

- A bloodied eye is a cause for concern because it may have injured itself.

- Cloudy eyes could be a hint of too much fat in its diet and domestically raised crickets can cause this - correction in diet is the best thing to do.

Care Sheet

Responsible pet ownership entails a number of conditions that you will need to meet. Rigid requirements of routine maintenance need to be carried out correctly and diligently. You will need to do these things in order for your frogs to thrive well.

Initially take care of the immediate needs, one of which is finding an experienced herp vet. Amphibians and reptiles are delicate beings to care for when in captivity. Improper or ill - informed care could spell immediate disaster for the little guys. A herp vet can help you sort out the details of proper amphibian maintenance.

When in captivity, it will be up to the amphibian keeper to provide the frog with a variety of proper, healthy and balanced food choices. The lack of food or improper food choices, will greatly compromise its health. The balance of nourishment may not result in immediate starvation but it will set off a host of health problems because malnutrition lowers the immune system.

Frogs thrive best on live crickets and mealworms, which can be purchased at your local pet shop. Crickets are the most common of food picks of keepers and should be the main staple of your frog's diet.

- Feed your frogs as many crickets and worms within a 15 minute period.

- Make sure that crickets are dusted with vitamins, calcium and necessary minerals.

- Make sure that the supplements you give the frogs appropriate and safe.

- Insects you feed the frogs should ideally be gut loaded.

- Insects with a tough exoskeleton can cause bowel impaction because these are indigestible

- Give your frogs superworms, king mealworms, earthworms and waxworms. Other insects which can occasionally be given for variety can be bought locally. Butterworms and silkworms can also be purchased online. Make sure that these meals are given live and set on the ground of the terrarium.

Tips on Feeding

- Never use your fingers to feed them

- Use a pair of tongs or tweezers

- Live bought prey needs to be eaten within 24 hours of the purchase

- Sprinkle vitamins and minerals on gut loaded insects for complete nourishment

Chapter Ten: The Ornate Frog and all the Species

There are eight species of the South American horned frogs and a few of them are easy to get, therefore, really popular amongst pet owners. Let's get to know them in this chapter so that you'll also learn the other species related to the South American ornate frog, and perhaps see if you want other quite similar species so that your pet can also have company should you choose to keep more than one frog pet.

Brazilian Horned Frog

Ceratophrys aurita is also known as the Brazilian horned frog or Wied's frog. The Brazilian horned frog is endemic to Brazil. It natural naturally occurs in subtropical or tropical moist lowland forests, freshwater marshes and ponds.

Colombian Horned Frog

Ceratophrys calcarata or better known as the Colombian horned frog or Venezuelan horned frog is found in Colombia and Venezuela. These frogs can be found in dry savanna, subtropical or tropical dry shrubland. They can also be found subtropical or tropical dry lowland grassland, as well as freshwater marshes.

Amazonian Horned Frog

Ceratophrys cornuta or the Surinam horned frog is also known as Amazonian horned frog. The Amazonian horned frog is a chunky amphibian that measures up to 7.9 inches. This big frog can be found in the northern parts of South America. It is a frog with an exceptionally wide mouth and it has horn-like projections above its eyes which are more pronounced than those of its close cousin's. Female Amazonian horned frogs lay up to 1,000 to 2,000 eggs at a time, securely wrapping the eggs around aquatic plants. This frog eats other frogs, mice, and lizards and insects. The tadpole of the Amazonian horned frog may attack each other as well as other tadpole species right after they are hatched.

Cranwell's Horned Frog

Ceratophrys cranwelli or Cranwell's horned frog is also known as the Chacoan horned frog. It is a terrestrial frog occurring naturally in the dry Gran Chaco region of Bolivia, Brazil, Paraguay and Argentina. Most adult species range from 3.1 to 5.1 inches long and can weigh up to 1.1 lb.

These frogs typically have dark green and brown coloration on their backs. Albino variants with orange and yellow backs also exist. The dark color scheme of the frog helps in hiding the animal as it burrows and waits for its next prey. They are aggressive eaters, even though they are typically inactive. These frogs are capable of leaping several body lengths to capture prey using their sticky tongue to latch onto prey and pull it into their mouth. These frogs are nocturnal. They sleep with their eyelids open. These are carnivorous amphibians that would eat frogs of the same or different sort. They would mostly feed on similar sized animals, and insects.

When exposed to extreme temperatures, these frogs would enter a period of estivation. This is when the frogs develop a thick layer of protective skin. This thick protective skin helps to trap moisture and aid in with the frog's respiration. Once the period of estivation is complete, the frog would then use its front and hind legs to remove the protective layer. The frog, often times, pull the skin over its back using its massive jaws. They would frequently consume the shed skin in the process.

The Chacoan horned frogs are very popular pets just like other Pacman frogs. Keep them in a humid environment, like a glass tank, layed down with moist substrate. Feed these Chacoan horned frogs a mixed diet of gut-loaded mice, earthworms, crickets, and feeder fish. These frogs must be fed every 1–2 days until it reaches 18 months. After this, these frogs should be fed once every 4–7 days.

These frogs are particularly susceptible to impaction because of their enormous mouths. This is a condition where the frog's gastrointestinal tract is obstructed by a foreign body. This can be almost anything, so make sure that there is nothing in the tank the frog would mistake for food. Nor should rocks be used as substrate because these can easily be swallowed by the Chacoan horned frog. Impaction usually leads to constipation and malnutrition. It can even cause death. Immediately treat with laxatives (get in touch with your vet or ask an experienced keeper). In severe cases, only expensive surgery is the option.

Caatinga Horned Frog

Ceratophrys juazeirense is also known as the Joazeiro horned frog and the Caatinga horned frog and naturally occurs in Brazil. It can be found in dry savanna, subtropical or tropical dry shrub land. The Caatinga can also be found in subtropical or tropical dry lowland grassland, and intermittent freshwater marshes.

Argentine Horned Frog

Ceratophrys ornata or the Argentine horned frog is also called the Argentine wide-mouthed frog or the ornate pacman frog. The Argentine horned frog is the most common species of horned frog that can be found in the grasslands of Argentina, Uruguay and Brazil. It has a big appetite and it is a fierce eater. This frog will attempt to swallow anything that moves too close to its wide mouth.

Insects, rodents, lizards and other frogs, are guaranteed goners.

Stolzmann's Horned Frog

Ceratophrys stolzmanni, the Stolzmann's horned frog or the Pacific horned frog is also known as Pacific big-mouthed frog. It is found in subtropical or tropical dry forests, subtropical or tropical dry shrub land, and the sandy shores of Ecuador and Peru. Its geographical range is very fragmented and is continuously shrinking due to human activities and intervention.

Ecuadorian Horned Frog

Ceratophrys testudo or the Ecuadorian horned frog is endemic to subtropical or tropical moist montane forests and intermittent freshwater marshes of Ecuador.

The Most Popular in the Trade

The C. cranwelli, C. ornata and C. cornuta are the most popular species in the pet trade, along with the captive-produced hybrid between the C. cranwelli and the C. cornuta, also known as the fantasy frog.

Index

Photo Credits

References

"Argentine Horned Frog" - Wikipedia.org

https://en.wikipedia.org/wiki/Argentine_horned_frog

"Basic Information Sheet: Ornate Horned Frog" – Lafeber.com

https://lafeber.com/vet/basic-information-for-ornate-horned-frog/

"South American Ornate Horned Frogs (Ceratophrys)" - KaieteurnewsOnline.com

https://www.kaieteurnewsonline.com/2017/01/15/south-american-ornate-horned-frogs-ceratophrys/

"South American Ornate Horned Frog" - SeaWorld.org

https://seaworld.org/Animal-Info/Animal-Bytes/Amphibians/South-American-Ornate-Horned-Frog

"Ornate Horned Frog: Stats & Facts" - AnimalPlanet.com

http://www.animalplanet.com/pets/other-pets/hornedfrog/

"Horned Frog Care Sheet" - TheAmphibian.co.uk

http://www.theamphibian.co.uk/horned_frog_care_sheet.ht
m

"The Pac – Man Frog with a Frig in its Throat" - BBC.com

http://www.bbc.com/earth/story/20150612-a-frog-with-a-
frog-in-its-throat

**"The Argentine "Pac Man" Horned Frog – Natural History
And Captive Care"** - ReptilesMagazine.com

http://www.reptilesmagazine.com/the-argentine-pac-man-
horned-frog--natural-history-captive-care/

"Common Illness in Pac Man Frogs" - PetHelpful.com

https://pethelpful.com/reptiles-amphibians/pac-man-frog-
health

"Argentine Horned Frog (Ceratophrys ornata)" -
ExoticPetVet.com

http://www.exoticpetvet.com/argentine-horned-frogs.html

"Frog Ornate Horned / Ceratophrys Comuta" –
Dudleyzoo.org.uk

http://www.dudleyzoo.org.uk/animal/frog-ornate-horned/

"Pac Man Frog / Ornate Horned Frog: Ceratophrys Ornata"
– BuffaloBirdNerd.com

http://www.buffalobirdnerd.com/clients/8963/documents/Pa
c_Man_Frog%20-%20ed%205-2014.pdf

"Choosing an Ornate Horned Frog" - PetPlace.com

https://www.petplace.com/article/reptiles/general/choosing-
an-ornate-horned-frog/

www.ingramcontent.com/pod-product-compliance
Lightning Source LLC
Chambersburg PA
CBHW062018040426

42447CB00010B/2053